A COLLECTION OF POEMS

THE MAN WHO DROWNED HIMSELF ON STAGE

PATRICK D. HART

NOTE FROM THE AUTHOR

I hope this book holds the fraying nerves of those reading it like a bouquet. None of us are alone. Not even when we think we are.

History

Is

Determined

By you.

And

By

How

Present

You

Keep it.

READER BEWARE

I read like the best parts of a novel
Trace your fingers down my spine
Pick apart the leaden parts of my mind
Breathe in this Armagedden from my lungs
I won't challenge your belligerent light
But beware of my poetic plight
You'll risk becoming a charitable gesture
That lingered too long in my desolate grandeur

SAVE

I'm always
Trying to save myself
By virtue
Of saving
Everyone else

A NAME

June came in wet wrists
A fistful of yellow Irish iris
I was nothing more than a blemished daisy
Pushed from your belly
A blade of grass shackled to winter
You named me Patrick
But "they" had different rally points
And I became every synonym for the word depression
As well as every antonym for the word love

Sometimes I look at the stars and wonder
If there is some galactic meaning
Something that cannot be explained by tides
Or creases in aged hands,
And
Occasionally when I look into the eyes
Of my best friends' son
I am a believer
But most days,
      Such as this Wednesday
      And every one that came before it,
      And after
I will look into the mirror and remember
There were several children born on my birthday
And all of their names rhyme with happiness
But you named me Patrick

WRITING IT OUT

Drenched
In time
And this stalemate
Spending aggressive hours lashing at your tongue
To set free those imprisoned and starving words

You spank those guilty thoughts
And smile at the thrill of holding hostages
Lay down and take two
Two arms, two legs, and two pints of insincerity

Yes—
I am insinuating that you're sick between the ribs
No one should enjoy hurting like this!

"That was music to my ears"

My manipulated years finally wrote a manifesto that
You can dissect and diagnose me with
Better you than some therapist
I tried that and ended up cleaner than she
But that's my cross to bear
A flash of something brilliant and manic
But labeled a disease

Disconnect your heart
Go ahead, I'll eat it
Candy comes in handy
During late night writers block
My brain needs increased insulin
How else do you think I survived?
It's time that I leave
If you promise to never forget
I'll promise to never remember saying it

THE GRAVE AND THE GROUNDSKEEPER

In my age
I have become defanged

Time tugs on my robe
As I luxuriate over the harm
That has begun to decay
Admittedly
The strokes of midnight hands
Often feel disrespectful
As if I'm ignorant
To the long coat of my shadow
Oblivious to the fact
That the past is such a jealous bride

With a long drag
I exhale the reckless ricochet of my old ways
I'm not ungrateful for the soil in my teeth
In fact
I can taste it after the third of fourth whisky
The flower bed that I mutilated with each sundial spin
Has shown me that none of us are malignant

I have always been
Both the grave and the groundskeeper
A dweller of distractions
Pulling daisies and the taste of licorice
From the conveniences of earthy groans

S N O W B A L L

Look mom, a bucket of clouds
They squish and swish around
And then you throw it at me
And smile

We didn't always fight nasty,
There were moments where we had fun
Moments where humans became more than,
Moments that turn people into angels
Or at least magnets
And seasons into memories
I kind of always feel like I'm courting a memory
A time
An instance
       it's Goddamn maddening

I grew up a lot after I fell in the wood
And you tended to my leg
I tried to tell you about the kid I hit with a hammer
The one that killed the old lady down the street
He smashed her pumpkin.
He smashed our pumpkin!
I got him! Mom, I got him!
You didn't hear me

At 8, I was talking about Vietnam with our 'crazy'
neighbor. He told me a lot more than my father
But he also gutted our pet cat
I hadn't seen the inside of love before that

Let alone really understand what love was
I suppose it has something to do
With seeing yourself splayed out on a tree stump
In front of inquiring eyes
It must have something to do with the feral beauty of
God and his inability to intervene with the healing
After seeing what humans reduce love to

Anyways,
I disposed of the cat so your daughter wouldn't have
to find it
I remember how you cautioned her about love
(I never got that talk)
I tried to tell you what happened to our pet
But you told me she just ran away
You made me a liar that day
But the balance of protection made that okay

T H O R N S

I can't
Hold onto
This pain anymore

It's like admiring a rose
While only
Clutching the thorns

DEVOTION, ALSO

Pain is a slow pour
Of something like honey or molasses
Just without any of the sweetness
Unless we are talking about devotion

You are the band aid on the wrist
Of a fourteen year old boy
Who just lost his brother in an accident

You are the phantom pain of a wounded Vet
Finding love in the ghost of trust
And the startling amount of focus it takes
To live without old patterns
Though you must

You are the empty stomach
Of a thirteen year old girl
Honoring her idols by becoming like them
She must starve for attention
Literally—
Starve for attention

You are the separate beds in separate rooms
And the married Christian couple in each of them
The garden side of love that became baron
From hunkering down in soiled troughs
Of many a putrefied season

You are the hunger of isolation
Like volume to the deaf
You are love for the dead

OPTIMIST, STAINED

I've been listening closely
To the sound of rain
Letting my self-awareness
Lose itself beyond the pane

Mother used to call me
Optimist, stained
And I always liked how it sounded
Coming from her mouth

Like my heart was a waxed flower
Born hopeful,
But without potential to grow

So I sit writing about bones I'll never own
Clink.
      Clink.
My left eye continues to twitch
Suddenly I've become a cloud
Floating—
Noticing animals below me
I crash into the sun and smatter my yolk

I'm helium
Pulling my roots from countries I never got to visit
And if there has to be a way to end
This. Is. It.

I'm coming to God with flowers
Un-waxed and full of mercy

He made such beautiful creatures
—Still, creatures
And that's a wound the womb doesn't learn

MARITIME ME

Truth is a terrible debt
It walks with its own four feet
And stretches further than the shadow
Of a skyscraper

In the garden of engorged prayer
I sit and feed the terrible things inside of me
Owning the voice that grovels
For a new skeletal
A new identity
And squirrel my face into something vulgar
Holding the wrong end of a wishbone

I was born a blue eyed Baptist
Who hurled himself into a pool of ink
With every desire to drown
But found it impossible to sink

So I speak of mirrors
Simply
To cut myself on the reflection
The wilting of my conscience
Is just the redux of a memory
Un-welcomed re-visitation

Balmy mouth
I begin

My body is a deserter
Ever since you steeped my grace in your hot breath

And entered my sand castle with the worst intent

Oh maritime me—
The waves came and went
Since I learned to hide inside this flesh
I've always felt connected to the sea

So here I am at the feet of a storm
Fingers stalking my wrist for a pulse
As my veins become sand
I take the ocean in my mouth
In large gulps
Until the siren takes my hand

<u>FIGHT</u>

Perhaps
In my next life
I will be someone
Who knows how to fight

Towards the end
Of this one though,
I will be happiest to know
That there are people
Who still live like that

THE MIRROR AND THE MICROSCOPE

Your father swapped his conscious
For the warmth of longer fingertips
It left you an alien
A table in your own house
A wilted flower in the middle of a drought

Your mother cried a lot
And worked even more
So much so,
That you never figured out why she came home
Smelling of booze and damage
You'd learn to relate to that in 15 years
You'd wear that smell so well
It was either nostalgia, or desire for an explanation
Sometimes the product no longer concerns itself
With the story behind it

Humanity is a lot like that actually

Your babysitter taught you more about the women
on the internet
And how to touch yourself properly
You never spoke about it.
Your sister needed you the way you needed your
brother.
The difference is not in letting go.
The difference is in how we let go of those letting go
of us when we are no longer needed

You needed you though.
You needed you so much that you built homes In a
million other fucking people

Swaddled by a definition
That was a series of easily chipped fingernails;
They always regrow, but differently
Slightly more fragile
Always, just slightly
And then you tried to kill yourself
It was tough to come to terms with
Harder to talk about
And harder still to write about.

It's overwhelming how much of this story you see in
everyone else
How much you feel the need to take their darkness
And place it inside of your own.
The mere fact that you even think
you can hold the worlds sadness is discerning

DEVOTION

I feast on the night
Adroit in the perching of my pen
Disregarding the reputed decision
Against hibernating in the nuclear self

I am the tension arc
I am the holy well
I am sputtering provocations
In a formidable dress code

Speak low.
Sink lower.
Until the chalice I inked in
Overflows.
Grave your ghost
While I raise my dead
The stems of this aggrieved palate
Refuse to regulate an indicted whim

There is warm havoc in my guts
Melting frozen courage in my lungs
I am an autumn tongue
Marauding crowds of poets
For penance and peace
Nothing of value comes with ease
I stand firm in the devotion to me

ADORN

It was dry air
A stale macabre of
Italian grape skin and apple rinds

The shame of saints
Aisled the allotment of sunlight
Through the window

If only we adorned our fears
The same way we do our beliefs

Beguiled by undercurrents
And the human soul
This body is content to contend with itself in the
shadows
And heave holy in the light

Go young humans
Own those creases
And dark smudges
In your skin
Trust the blessing you were born in

MONSTER

You created a monster
Out of your sadness

I made a lover
Out of mine

LOVE, HURT, HAPPINESS

Love calls me a whore
Stationed between two trees
I stand fickle
Like a jilted promise
And its power to bring either pillar
To its knees

Hurt calls me a junky
Scouring ten thousand roses
Collecting all the thorns
To press into my palms
And quote scripture
The way my mother would
It didn't work then
And it won't work now

Happiness calls me a liar
Some grandeur left in the other house I was born in
The one providing new paint
For a loyal family

> *It feels less like home*
> *And more like an orphanage*

SADNESS, MY CONCUBINE

Tenderize my wit
There's a clock in the distance
Counting down the moments
And one day I'm going to stop staring at it

Oh sadness, my concubine
I won't apologize
For defending my famine

You ride in on a pale horse
Pretending to be magic
For the artists
Saying,
"Keep cutting it out of you, you'll get better soon,
I promise"

But you're just growing a cancer to harvest

TO BE NOTHING AND EVERYTHING

I am all things to all people all the time
While synchronically
Being nothing
To no one, ever

This is art
A jellied jowl resting on the
Thinning edge of a solar eclipse,

Expose your weakness
The blue pool jazz blemish
Let your hands bleed all over me
O'
Give me your cheap honeymoon progeny
Uncharted blasphemy
Spoken like a tongue turning in a lock
Swirling the pit out of a peach
With such poetic speech

This is the brilliance of meaninglessness
The vestige of dusk
It takes a tidal wave of black
To swallow this kind of pain
And you will never know
The vertigo
Felt by staring at your moon

Let the color run
Disorient and then gravitate your spine
Correct the suspension
And collapse

This is art.
We are now
And never

E S T U A R Y

You are an
Estuary of goodness
And so much more
Than orphaned bones
You simply must believe in them
To give yourself a home

EMPATH

Slumped over in roaring traffic
The hum of huffing machines
Clamoring and clunking
I understand them
I was born with too much fucking empathy
I lend my heart to everything
And my lungs breathe emotions
Into deities
As I worship at the feet
Of those false mountains
Without giving but a thought
To the eventuality
That they will topple over me

A N X I E T Y

Damn
Here I am again
At the bottom of a swimming pool
Looking up at the belly of a continent
Pushing waves against the current

All these memorials and monuments
Are fixed inside the eyes of people dying
Why do I see their guts?
Am I the only one?

I hide out in quadrants
Of ceiling tiles
And checkerboard floors
I lock myself in bathroom stalls
Twice every ten minutes
Just trying to make sense of this
I'm so fucking anxious

These skeletons are laughing at me
For having such thin skin
Each one telling me to join them
What's funny though—
>   *They are all just ghosts*
>   *Of all my past reflections*

God built me a home
Inside of his mansion
But I was in the library
While everyone else was watching television

I know I can't stay here. I can't give up
Lights. 12 spiders, a fly—half eaten
Like me.
Here.
In this place.

It's a maze of colored fabrics out there
And I am made of feathers
While they are all made of fists
I can't overcome this
I will overcome this
I can overcome this
I ___ overcome this.

ORANGE

I used to believe
That I was an onion
With all those layers

Now I know
With absolute certainty
That I am an orange
With a sticky rind

PIKES PEAK

There's a wafting of honeysuckles
Raking my fingertips against
Childhood soil
My eyes count rivers that look like veins
From miles above
Yet still—
In these spoils
I ache like a stone in a jetty

There is a lavender tear
Winding down the cheek
Of Pikes Peak
I wonder of the feet that paved the path
For such a view

Age and beauty
Have no place in monuments
Simple bravery is displayed
By standing upright
In spite of time
Often
I regret teaching my trembling body so much
From the carved and mute
But today—
My marks appreciate the tools used
To create something so astute

I am mortified by the fact that
I am a martyred reflection in God's junkyard
Breathing fabled and heavy
Though I realize this stone in the jetty
Is covered in His flood
Un-drained
Protected by some kind of bountiful love

Minutes ago I was ready
To turn blush to a simple sunrise above
And give up
But now, I shall stay
A monument
If not just for one more day

TEENAGE WRISTS

A treasure of convenience
Like ice in your glass
On a summer day
I am a teenage wrist
Wet with mistakes
Unable to comprehend
Our contract with time

I am fine
I am fine

I am insecure
Though I am sound
Embarrassed by the fragility
Of my presence on stage
With teeth that never fit the boy
And mental health that never fit the man

Call it a phase
Call it a phase

Until thirty years later
Acceptance holds the hands of grief
And I am entangled with the muse that created me
Symbiotically
I am happily married
But belong to the seductive legs of misery

I wilt
With a belly full of woe
Waiting for the right mouth
I have become a cliché
Begging to be saved
Yet I worship nothing enough to pray

I ache to ache
Just never quite enough to break

DIM STARS

The truest stars I know
Do not shine nor glow
They tremor with trophy light
That lodges inside
Some bereaved river that swells
Against the shore it beats against
Creating thick mud
And with a mouth full of muck
They still speak
Valiant truths of love

INNOCUOUS FLOWER

Glory malts and you are the afterbirth
Alone on a hillside
A one armed scribe on this palisade
Bridging the gap between
Guile speech and warrant belief
From this curious tabernacle

You won't become a tree
And you don't need to be
Colorful little seed blooming
Proud petals arranging
Like a dream catcher
You summit my rutted nightmares
Offering bountiful blessings
Like loneliness is prosthetic
And depth doesn't have to be poetic
Sometimes hurt just does and is

The only quandary surrounding love
Is the way we mate with humility

Innocuous flower
If ever something further from ineffectual
Existed—
It is you.

BAODING BALLS

I do not know who influences me
I am not a student of poetry
I rip my eyeballs from my face
And swirl them
Like Baoding balls
Smearing my digestion on each page

I regurgitate the good parts of this pain
And it pains me to admit
That I am not okay
But I am getting better at writing about it

I didn't ask for ghosts
They started as my neighbors
And now they are living inside my home
It's anyone's coffin I guess
And I won't dispose of company

Death is a contact high
For people like me
We dream
And idolize
But it is not interesting or fun
To always feel like you are burying yourself
In moments
And not be able to tell the difference
Between heavy eyes and late nights

I used to be so cavalier
Before
Death was a decoration on my memory
But now it fuels me
Beyond compare

I know that
Nothing green can stay
I am loyal to the grief inside of me
There is a triumph to love
Because of its mystery
But I sleep well knowing
I can make sense of my misery

<u>ORCHIDS</u>

Loneliness grows like a weed
Where love—
Love blooms like an orchid
It must be nurtured kindly

MUTUAL LOVE

My father said to me,
Son, one day
You'll be a shiny rock
Formed by the pressures of the earth
Some girl will look at you
In a way
That makes it hurt a little less
She'll want to wear you
On her promise finger,
And Son
It will not work between you two
Unless you understand
That she was forged
From the same pressures too

THE DAY I KNEW

I remember the temperature of the room
When I let you in
Not through the door, but to a place reserved
For more monsters and less humans.
It took a few drinks, but I wasn't too drunk
To remember those loose blue overalls
With the left strap undone.
Or the way your eyes said,

*"Don't worry, we're not going to press our walls together
Just to see what crumbles."*

I intentionally wore those short shorts to see how
you would deal with scars from self-harm,
And it came from a place of unrecognizable love.
Maybe unfamiliar is a better word; unfamiliar to me
anyways.
We didn't kiss.
We hardly touched; physically.

I was mystified by your honor. I was turned on by
your laugh. You spent exactly 12 minutes planting
light shards In my dark garden of self-idealizing
suffering. It was opposite of all the cliché saying and
movies where goosebumps burst from cold skin.
The temperature rose. I felt hydrated again.
You were my moon and tides in me were rising.

From that moment I knew that the world could keep
its love songs. It could grasp tightly to its ballads and
Valentine's Day monuments
I would no longer need them.

M O R N I N G

I may not be able to touch your hand
But I find you in the meter of the morning
And commit the songs I sing
To the moments
That I may be too honest to be inspiring

There are colors pouring
Like a thunderstorm through a kaleidoscope
When you visit me in a daydream

It's both crushing
And uplifting

MY WIFE

She wants to know
How I make myself cry
    I never tell her

It's the inadequacy I stitch to my heart
Little by little each day
It's the way I think about
Running into traffic
Because some people age into depression
While mine was crib crawling

That's a confession I've never made

She wants to know
How I make myself cry
    I never tell her

It's how my mother's love
Turned patience into a sparkler
And sent colors of the rainbow
Crashing into raging seas below

It's how the product of a divorced family
Was just the beginning
It was the misconception of love
And how it actually has nothing to do
With loyalty or promise

She wants to know
How I make myself cry
    I never tell her

How death gave distance definition
How I struggle to feel anything
As strongly as loss
And that's the problem

She wants to know
How I make myself cry
But honestly—
It's the thing that keeps me from crying most nights
That she should want to know

It's her.
Only her

NEXUS OF MY HAPPINESS

You are the nexus of my happiness
I hope that you
Always feel smothered
By the damp fog of my persistence

My love
I want my love
To coat you like a million drops of rain
And if I have to belong to a body
I hope it's a body of water
I hope it's yours

I want to paint you in pastels
And hear you plagiarize my name
Over morning coffee

You are devoid of flaws
When you abandon your clothes
And stand in front of me
I'm always staring—
Busy picking cotton candy
From between your teeth

This love feels like fame
And I want to help all those sad songs
Forget your name

You are the nexus of my happiness

THE ART OF OUR BODIES

I'm not an artist
I cannot paint with my hands
The way I can with my speech
Unless I'm in bed with you
Then Rembrandt and Van Gogh
Would take notes from me

Centuries of love makers
Would be lost
Attempting to forge
The art of our bodies

I'm all hands
When I'm tangled in your kind of poetry

TWO VOLCANOES

Your body is poetry
And I need it
The way it needs me

You are scented like familiar Sundays
Melting on my tongue
Like button candy

I bathe in the glow of your eyes
Nothing but a message in a bottle
Making love to the moonlight

And together
We are the sound of two volcanoes
Pressing against one another
A diatribe from stubborn angels
Shooting arrows at the sphere
That burned and shamed us
Both mad and blue
Until we segue into
A melody of porch swing wind

We make love with all lips and limbs
And then talk about it
In whispers,
As if tonight is the night that the world ends

Little porcelain
My beautiful and broken
It is time for us to Wed
And for the stillness that has been suppressed
In our lungs for so long
To swirl and rage together
It is time to belong

Your body is poetry
And I need it
The way it needs me

LITTLE DEVOTIONAL

Speak to me
In flagrant harmonies
Give me a reason to believe
In a love that stands like a sequoia
Or reaches across the Baltic Sea
To some Grecian castle where dreams
Are kept in music boxes

There are grooves in your smile
That I haven't yet explored
A short detour down your naval
To a foreign shore
Wet with desire and reason to abandon
The circumference of our peripheral dreams
Our bodies circumflex

I will not love you in moments
I shall do it in deep breaths
In a devotional scapular

You are a promise that I shall not evict

THE SECRET TO LIFE IS DEATH

I see her trying to figure me out sometimes
Wondering how my coping looks like resiliency
And I want to tell her the trick is
To see everything as dead
Which is understandably sad
And I know if she hears it
Mountains will fall to dust between her ribs

I don't want to remove the sparkle from her eyes
Though the truth is
I rationalize
And categorize
Preventing pain by keeping it all artificial

This is no way to live
But it is how to survive

I keep this all a secret
Including the fact that
She is the first thing I have allowed my hands to
touch
That made me believe
They might be capable of growing something

I'm scared to death to let my secret slip
Because if I allow the dam to splinter
I'll dry up
And be nothing more than another lonely poet
Damned to resent her

DEPRESSION AND ITS CHILDREN

Breathing heavy through my cheeks
Counting backwards
To the last cigarette I smoked last week

I ingest too much caffeine
So I'm able to think
But really it's the guilt of living
That's harassing my heartbeat

Here we go again
Forsaking my mental health
Not forgiving myself
Drowning in the rain
Because I won't lower my head
Or close my fucking mouth

I remember a time
When I'd say
I want to play in traffic
"Don't worry Hun,
I'm just being poetic"
But now my thinking has evolved
To how the kids will remember it
A multi-fractured body
Laying in the casket

It's all become too real
It's gotten too heavy

My heart is making demands
My brain starts making plans
I'm running the bathwater
I'm running the bathwater again

Who said you can't see the devil in the dark?
It's the only time I see his eyes
So I sleep with a bible to my right
And a gaudy ceiling light

Oh, porosity
You can't fix me
I know these blue eyes
Make it seem easy
But I promise they've swallowed
More hearts than I'd like to admit

A kind saint is just an easy target

HIGH ON LOVE

Nothing lasts forever baby
So let's get high

Forget our weight
And the weight of the crashing world

We're all just waves
Repeating and reaping
Sick homes to sicker feelings

All I want to do
Is exist with you
In a cloud
So we can look down
On the lost souls
Feigning for love
Forcing wishbone breaks
And say
I would never trade that for this
Not now
Not any day

RO T A T I O N

Forgiveness is found in the cooling of blatant heat
A treasure typically reserved for hunters and priests
Finally shifting in the form of falling leaves
A light reprieve
From hollow hell and dampened glory

The sky awakens to bodies succumbing
To the Cliff Swallow's song
A disbelief of patience
That strands the torture of constant war
For beauty is a season in desire
  It is a body bright in the fingers of sunlight
And a bored man's tongue
Still finds the fruits of passion
In the throes of such calm illumination

Roadside Maples dance in irenic fashion
With acorn offerings
Littering the feet of wolves nurturing the day
And autumn prints pry fault from
The aging quay of the mind

Alas, the first of its kind bows
To the womb of a sunrise
As dusk falls
The earth becomes a beautiful woman behind the
glow of her cigarette
And I—
A statue on a mantle watching her glory echo

TRAGEDY

Tragedy finds us all
In time—
Even in defiance of it

TO DIE KNOWING LOVE

Please live
To feel enough pain
To die
Knowing love

Honestly—
There is no
Greater understanding
Or feeling

DEFINING DEATH

Death is a widower
An impetuous griever
And the almighty deceiver

PINK ROSES PT.3

I don't know what to do with my hands anymore

I used to smoke
But I quit
Because you hated the way
It changed how I tasted

I used to pick at my fingernails
And when they bled
You would hold me and say

"Babe, you don't have to show the world how you
feel inside"

You understood me that way
So I quit
I wanted to show you that I was repairing

I used to hold your hand
On long drives and
Through late nights
It replaced all these things I did
With once un-important hands

And then it happened
An unbalancing
The unraveling
A drunk driver singing songs
To his broken heart
Broke mine
And the only things these hands are good for any-
more
Is bringing pink roses to your grave

I don't know what to do with my hands anymore
I don't know what to do with my hands anymore

5TH STAGE OF GRIEF

Bring your cheekbones to your eyes.
        Bring your cheekbones to your eyes.

I heard it so many times that it stopped being clever.
Now that you are gone, I do it every day
Until my muscles spasm
Matching the soreness in my heart.

Maybe I'm just trying to feel closer to you.
The truth is when I get home
I pet the dog and let my cheekbones droop
Until I look like that shaggy Shar-pei you left behind
The luggage is down, and I can breathe.
Two fingers in a glass. I stare at pixels, or read a
book.
One where the main character has your name.
It's easier this way, and in short spurts
I can feel you sitting by my side.

All of a sudden the cheekbones are to my eyes.
I didn't even mean to this time.

<u>SURVIVING</u>

I've been surviving
       Not in a colorful way
But not like a hoax either

I've been making my bed in the morning
And noticing things
       Like the fragrance of coffee

I've been downsizing
Throwing out the could-have-been's
And since-then's
       I've been surviving

I've been exercising
Sweating more
Detoxing
       Yet I still feel your twisted tongue
Spun around my strengthening lungs

I've been taking more showers
       Baths presented
Drowning as a choice
       So I'm changing what I can
       I'm owning this voice

No requiescat for the old me
The one decomposing in the bed I made this morning
I am surviving

PINK ROSES PT.4

Panicked dreams of drugged out patterns
With you in every piece of light
Reflecting off of the kitchen floor

The old days are gone
And that has me concerned
Convinced that persistence
Gets us somewhere further away—
Yet it's not any further away from the distance

My knees buckle
Holding the weight of this coffee cup
Your hands used to curl around the ceramic
This is the only way that I can still wrap my fingers
around yours

I don't think this is depression
It is love—
For I cannot let you go

The dramatics in my circulatory system
Are keeping me from doing something awful
More awful anyways—
You see I am doing awful things
To keep from doing awful things
I think you understand me

I hate spending time with my shrinking reflection
But it hurts less to talk to God
When I feel like I am moving towards Him

I'm met with echoes in my latency
Yet still—
There is victory in this vacancy
For when all this room exists
There is space for it to be filled with love
In spite of my depravity

MERCY

Mercy is the love
That casts anguish from a heart

The trilogy of a stare
That brings the jewel of June to May
It is as foolish as it is rare

Watch the breath of a daylily bloom
At the husk of daytime
Knowing it was worth
Its only taste of sunlight

Mercy will exalt the graceful
And exhaust the dim
It is rejuvenation

Mercy is both death and creation

F O R W A R D

Like oxygen leaving a room full of ghosts
It's always about sealing wounds
The anticipation and anxieties
That leave me a pile of skin
With one leg in my underwear
At the bottom of the mattress

Then that jaw break sunrise
Rises somewhere in the Far East
Calling out—
Upon some mountain
My spine stands plumb in its presence

But really
It's never the places that free us at all

So smoke summer, filter-less
And if you must run
Do so toward an avalanche, fearless

Mercy is just a tourist
Inside of a song
And if you exhale too long
You will dissolve
Before you learn how to belong

LIFE AND DEATH

Death is
More about life
Than we admit

Look around
You'll see it

FAMILY

Sister—
There's so much skin
On your teeth still
I have seen all of the things
Dying inside
Come to life at one time
And I want to see you
Survive all the little deaths
You have witnessed in your short life

Brother –
You already traded that smile
For Southern Grape Ferns
And at least I continue
To see hope in how they grow
Though you never told me
That we were building everything
Out of borrowed time
I love you still for the time
You gave me

Mother—
I saw you yesterday
In the madness that erupted
From my voice
It came from a place unwashed
Where you raked fingernails
Of truth
Along the soft creases of my cheek
You jackhammered this fuse into me
During ossification
And on my trip down the well
I saw the face of my planted seeds
And realized that pain and love
Can be delivered,
        and digested separately

Father—
You gave me your eyes
And it hurts
To love the world this much
I love you
I will always understand

YEARS LATER

Tar in my mouth
It sits lukewarm in the mind
I scribble rapidly
Writing the ghost of Saint Michael out of me

I'm drowning

It's not just sleep
But rather the county shutting down
And the lack of the eulogy
I was drunk and you transmogrified
Before my eyes
From becoming to never became

Fried food and punk rock
Skating on the frozen lake
In your backyard
Cigarette dreams that honestly
I'm still smoking

Quitting seems disrespectful

My eyes welled for the first time in too long
And I seemed shy to them
It was a warm pain
Something deeply dissenting—
Here I am
Older than you will ever be
Listening to records you'll never hear
Realizing

That I am a ripple in a universe that
Without your gravity
You are somehow still creating

Swollen honeycomb brain
Take me away
And swallow me into that fencing breeze
I'll keep you warm like coffee
Cheap company
And murmur mournfully
When the tar sits lukewarm in my mind

FIVE YEARS AND COUNTING

Today I am rolled over
Mauled by bitter sundown
And the amalgamation
Of sterile interaction and dulled colors

What did I miss?
Was it the phone calls?
Or the way you would have to clinch your jaw
To utter "God" through your teeth?
Was it the rusting way you would say goodbye

I was too busy honoring your strength
To acknowledge your misery

I remember the parking lot at 8pm
When you left us for Alaska
You told me to look after my sister
(Which I'm failing at)
Was the ground vibrating and I missed it?
If you come back,
I swear that I would feel it
I would stop you

Today I am worn
Like the carcass of trees
And the cigarette burning
So closely
I am dried wood
I am dyed wool
And I am weak enough
To light the whole thing myself

Pennywise, smokes, and Jameson
Today is about recognizing that love
Comes in many forms
And sometimes we dirty our hands
With devotion to the glacier inside
And man, you burned so goddamn bright
That the ice melted too soon
And I forgave you long ago,
But it scares me to admit
That I understand you
That I understand It

There's a lack in the air
Hands reach up from soft soil
As my head ascends
My body repines
Fawning eyes used to hold me
Until the things inside
Became a sadness you couldn't teach
It has been five years and counting

FRAGILE PEOPLE

The most
Fragile people
I have ever met
Are the ones
Who claimed
To be anything but delicate

GROWTH

The smell of citrus under cerulean clouds
An ode to bubblegum
Sticking to the backside of my canine teeth

There is a piece of you
In that spritzed morning grass
From the sporting field
That stays stained to my knees
A memory
That admittedly has its own discrepancies
Yet still—
It belongs to me

Nature has clay feet
The depth of which pays no attention
To Sunday's like these
For the world was busy being built
Long before my ancestors thought of words
To describe the loss of everything
They sought out to achieve

You disappear like watercolor
But your voice—
It resounds so clear
Like infinite spring
Or the mist of a sprinkler that never really dries
From the labyrinth of the ear
Call on life
And the warmth of colors

Bring me the moisture of levity
  Return to the days when love
  Had hands attaching islands
  Instead of balled fists
  Irrigating the space between them

Make it all cosmic again
A speck, a fleck, an atom of creation
The more infinitesimal, the better the chance
To allow wonder to enter

Rise like heat in those waterstone bones
Feel the buoyancy
Feel the possibility
Feel everything
Everything distancing from that sticky memory

Growth supervenes the opportunity of a new beginning
Not from the preservation of an ending

FIND LIGHT

I found sadness in my
Mother's knuckles
And behind my father's smile

Sometimes
It hits you for no reason

Sometimes
Despite the sun
You can't find the light

It is important to remember
That it is going to be alright

HARDEST TIMES

Still heavy
After all these years

But I have learned
If we can give the same flowers to graves
That we give to brides

Then we can honor ourselves
Even through the hardest of times

ONLY THE BRAVE EAT

Mason jars arranged
To catch the rain
Our tongues rimmed the edge
Fighting our fathers for space

Classic winters and classic cars
Couldn't create men
From impoverished salesman

To think:
I just wanted you to take me to find time
Instead we found tobacco row
And I was issued dreams
Where all I see anymore
Is black smoke

Lukewarm coffee drinks like stolen youth
It reeks of failure and evidence
The whooping cough never vaccinated against
History is nothing more than fattened consequence
   Son--only the brave eat
It's something you said numerous times
It still rings like the unveiling of colors at sunrise

"Kitsungi" was taught differently to me
Replacing melted gold with a gin wash
And tarred realism
That muck was baked in
Either that, or
Some seeds have thorns
And your seed is me

So now
At the precipice of life
I set my trident tip
Firmly in the gut of every adjacent person
To ensure I am the first to see the landscape
From the summit

THE SADDEST PART

There is a letter than needs to be read
Wedged in a wallet behind your photo
Stuck to some expired credit card
It says,

"I won't end up like you. Don't do it, stay alive."

But it's hard to
Because there is something genetic
About this condition
   Though we can never prove it

I sleep with no guns in the house
And always have a witty response
As to why,
But at night
My soup can scars have conversations
With these chewed fingernail beds
And they know better

I didn't acknowledge it 100 days ago
Not aloud anyways
And it's the first time in 4 years
That I didn't listen to that song
Playing on the radio
When the call came that you snuffed out your light

I remember how differently the world looked at that
moment
I swear I've been mostly color blind since
You didn't get to see me turn thirty
You didn't get to see me get married
You didn't get to see everyone you loved
Loving you so strongly
And that's the saddest part

WARM GUTS OF SUMMER

There is pressure in reach
It devours me
A helpless ache from able bodies
That smuggled hell into heaven
Under the saintly names they were given

There is a fury that cannot be taught
It bursts like the sun
Unharnessed
Wanton
Understood only by the pride of abandonment

It is attention we seek
Yet affliction we keep
Numbered by tepid tongues
Begging for a river to plunge in
With winter mouths still sucking
At the warm guts of summer

CELL PHONES IN HEAVEN

I am the rib of Adam
A transplant taking a thimble stock
Of who I am during winter's eve
Wearing white to the funeral party
Witnessing the death of a year of disbelief

It has been a while since I've seen God
I think I smoked him up
At some High School party
But that was 10 years ago
And my brother and I
Could still share a pint
Before chewing packs of gum all the way home
So we didn't reek of pubescent boredom
And I sometimes wonder
What could I have done differently?

I've seen so many things since

People start to look the same
When you spill enough of your blood
In different countries
I move after I can name six rows of streets
Because familiarity is company kept by colonies
And I subscribe to no King

Not anymore

I still get those headaches
The ones that welcome loneliness
In a way that differs from anxiety
And I still hate the ocean
But it's different

I used to be afraid to drown,
Now I'm afraid I'll do it intentionally

(I still find so much that is ugly in the cavities of the
strangers I meet. And with these hands I used to
give a damn! Like I could repair hate, and kick the
shit out of bullies. Like I could do what you did, and
make people feel less alone. The world has changed
so much man, I'm sure you know. I just can't call to
talk about it with you on the phone.)

THE FALLACY OF MANKIND

Through my nose,
I took everything I could
To make the ache
In my head stop

There were yellow whales
And pipers wearing polka dots
Pretending to be God
The devil held a sword
Like the archangel he was
And threatened the weather

Isn't it something
When the thunder of a father
Is challenged by the tide of a son;
Yet free will bought mankind the moon?

I challenged traditional thought
By letting the animals in my stomach out
Vampires in white cloth told me my penance
Led to something called a blood clot
And every voice in the room
Sanctioned by love
Was suddenly divided
By their bindings to strength
Empathy
Or necessity

I learned
That color matters
And that humanity classified everything
Including the intangibles
So we could create crowns
For crowded rooms

But when we simplified faith
We lost his name
And now his face only shows
In the most Ungodly Place(s)
Give me happiness or death
But dammit, let love rest

RECOVERY

My ribs are no good for me
All your arms resembling teeth
I write because it's safe
And I don't want you touching me

I've been there
        Wrestling doubts
Building structures on something
Sinking,
        Surrendering
To replica youth

I survived a thousand cuts
Just to die on a thousand and one

No one ever tells you about *that* one

The one that comes after the moment
That you're supposed to be better

Recovery isn't a promise
It's progress
A loss of purpose that you fill
With a different purpose

DEFINING AGING

Our youth is promiscuous in nature
Not yet long toothed
So we calcify our habits
And naively ignore our growing bones
To keep room for tempos
Checked frequently
By sex drives and carotid arteries

Our love is made hateful
Only by time
The waves that drown clouds
As fluorescent lights give orchards
Their names

It's the way we define good
By how much good we've done
I can taste it all

Aging is particular
It is always slow enough to count
The steps
But only after
You've traveled too far
To start again

OLD HOUSE

I was born and raised
In an old house
It creaked
When I would sneak around
It swayed and moaned
In ways
That kept me awake
> *I used to hate that old house*

I woke with an early exhale today
And my back hurt
These bones felt more like pins
That I drug around with opposition

I am nothing now
But a bedlam of ambition
Salivating for a younger body
Able to kiss courage once again

I yearn for a temple to pray
That knows no shame

I am an old house
I only hope that
I don't take this body for granted now

I AM

I am a humble abstract
A quote from Don Quixote
That breathes life into the pathways of the mind
I am a valiant palate
Allowing the taste of you
To vibrate down my spine
I am all parts of a hopeful heart
That lost a bet to the strength of time

I am a mountain peak in an arctic range
Untouched by human eyes
Like a lunar ghost on a careful day
The afterimage of recourse
Which gives frame to decency after remorse

We are unconditional
A pageantry of tilted lips
And I am your centerfold
The lust at noirs fray

I am the dulling blade in the gut of the day
The prophetic poetry that parts your lips
As if you heard something you had
Always wanted to say
I am a fortress
But I am a moat
And I will let you love my skin
If you can accept the person within

LIMBS

The sad thing
About my limbs
Is they will disconnect
And wrap themselves
Tightly around old pain
Before trusting
That love
Has the ability to forgive

FAIRYTALES

I think the truth is
That we treat love
Like it's pretend
Because we learned
About it from Fairytales

DEPRESSION IS AN EDIBLE DESIRE

Like warming fruit
Your cigarette arms
Are heating my body

It reminds me of a younger kitchen
When my pulp was less patient
But now your coffee eyes
Lingering on mine
Leave my tongue salivating
For your sanctuary

I remember the one before you
Said, "Depression is an edible desire"
And I told myself
"Believe nothing from that liar"
But often,
            We starve ourselves from the truth
And I know,
Strictly from the state I'm in
That I am eating for two

THE SOUL WILL MAKE YOU
A MARTYR OF LOVE

I'm going to bury you in cursive
And other things that died out
When I was young enough
To remember their purpose
But too old to forget
How they made me feel
Learning them for the first time

You sit like confetti
On a damp floor
An abhorrent collection
Of over celebrated victories

I'm just a straight spine
I'm just fixed teeth
I'm just thin skin
Wriggling inside of a lion's den

I may be patient
But the soul will make you
A martyr of love
And time will make us all
Deviants in the end

You see
Hope is an apology to oneself
It's soft fingers over raised cuts
On a thigh
That healed just enough

PLUM WINE

Plum wine was nothing more than amateur love
Some kind of distancing technique

I used to pretend you were meant for me
A cliché puzzle piece
But the truth is you were coating
And cloaking
The medicine I needed to hit bottom
So I could recognize what I was worth

You are the broken heart metronome
Hostage to a filthy box
Held by well-endowed boys that you shall never love
Yet always exist to

Congratulations—in fact
I hope you revel in the fact
That you are the last person I ever lied about

Iron and words
The grit in my gums
That I let assimilate my taste buds
To the texture of blood

The sex, the fear, the 'love'
Unpalatable and flecked in your skin
You hold enough for the both of us
Until your death is celebrated
And to the universe
Some other temptress
Is born again

THE LAMENT OF A HOPEFUL TONGUE

I just kept tonguing grapefruit
Like I did when I was twelve
Trying to get used to
Sour bites and red eyes
Without flinching

I evolved my practice
To pears and melon
Curing them with sugar first
Though my technique was improving
There was something missing

Some paradises desire a God
But spend eternity trying to find one

Then I got a taste
Of the hate between your legs
For a world that took advantage
Of a sweet heart
It began a slow rot
A decomposition of love
That dripped
      And dripped
            And fermented impolitely
Oh familiarity
Oh nostalgia
Oh understanding

I will love your depression double chin
Maybe then—
Together,
We can change the flavor
Of our disposition

CHEAP DEMANDS

This body is a charming disguise
Which withers like winter flowers
When it looks into the mirror

Pull me apart with your lips
Or your hands
Or your words

Make those cheap demands
And ask me to push into you
In a way that will leave your body charred
With bits of my aura

Nothing tells me what to do
Louder than silence

DUALITY AND THE CREDITORS OF EACH

I'm fucking sick and tired
Of seeing my roots
In every customer
I guess there is no sanctuary
For my well hung branches
That flourish inside
Only the most prodigious mirror

The depth of which
My darkness
So quickly becomes your prison

With every violent violet cactus kiss
You beg for my storm
Though I feed off of your drought

These atoms aren't seasonal delight
With Freudian refusal to appeal
To your mothers abandonment

We fight at dawn
To triumph this tragedy
Only to bow at its feet
At night

Tiny gaslight
Keep me warm
Self-awareness doesn't come cheap anymore
We must sell
Every bit of our dignity
To hold but an ounce of pride

FEAR NOT

My dear
I was edging
Up my spear
Until you
Taught me
That love
Is the purpose for—
Not the product
Of fear

FEAR OF LOVE

We work out in the dark
Ashamed that we might find love
In the way our bodies move

The fear of love is something
We hold dear
It's a first tattoo
It's coming so close to death
That you feel alive
       Alas—the gamble of time

The worst parts of myself have been carved
From a nightmare you once had
Before I was born
And now I'm sewn together
With skin from foreign lovers
In some attempt to find you
Under the covers
Or in the mirror

Something beautiful is thumbed
Into the fabric of this earth
But it cannot be me
For I am discarded rose leaves collecting
Consecrated grapes fermenting

LESSONS FROM SEASONALITY

I implore you
To carve through
Soft hearts

To be a conduit
For those too easy
To seek adventure

Be the way
That summer
Makes people remember
That milk thistles are beautiful

But please
Harbor turbulence
Like winter storms
Learn from that intense freeze

Our marrow can learn resiliency
From the fragility
Of seasonality

LOVE YOURSELF

Teach yourself how to love
Each part of you
No matter how small
Before someone comes along
And tells you what parts
Are worth loving
Or not loving at all

BEAUTY

You will grow to miss
The things you find insignificant
The linear value of beauty
Is held *not* in a single moment

JOY

Take me dancing
Where my sacrifices
Can meet yours
Where we can diagnose
How to downsize pupils
And calm heart beats
Of the strongest beasts

Take me to that room
Where the rest of the universe
Doesn't exist
Let me feel again
How it felt to be acknowledged
By shadows swallowing shadows

The kiss of someone else's depression
Is more light than I ever deserved

Take me to that place
Where trust isn't primitive
Where I remember what it is like
To hold something infinite

I left you there
When I crawled out of the moons craters
I left you there
An orphan
Born with their mothers tongue muttering
That—
Joy is nothing more than that of a first name
Singing in the rain

MOTION

My love is cumbersome
Trust me
It may taste good, though—
My doomsday will leave an echo
Between your legs
It will last as long as our bodies have gravity

Oh maniacal me
Those heavens are so deep
So I shall bury myself in things
Until God speaks back to me

And during
We will own every sin
The lights are on
And the physicality is beautiful

I will balance you on my chin
So I can taste the seismic activity
From your eruption

Gentle is a good night
Something forgiving
But when our bodies are colliding
We want to feel the ocean rising

Together we will beat back the dark
That spent decades engulfing two hearts

<u>F L O W E R S</u>

She loves flowers
None really in particular. Which is somewhat ironic,
Considering she is anything other than,
"Nothing in particular."

Roses were fine. Potted and wild Tulips.
Magnolias, both southern and Chinese.
Things that grew on vines,
And climbed higher than the knees of children.
Flowers were beautiful and she admired beautiful
things.

I tried to give her flowers once,
Cut and arranged by my own hands.
But my gift was met by such disapproving eyes.
I did not understand. She loves flowers.
How could she not love these?

It took time to understand. A few days,
Consisting mostly of me moping.
Boxing madness within my own mind.
A mid-June afternoon opened my eyes
To where I had gone wrong.

She loves flowers, because they were beautiful in
their blooming.
They were beautiful in their life cycle and season.
To remove such gentle growing things, and set
Their bodies on a desk
Was not just restrictive.
But it subjected her soul to watching beauty die.

Next time I want to surprise my wife
I will give her a garden to grow

BODIES IN THE DARK

I am fashioned by midnights and songs
Inspired by half crushed sand castles
Still standing close to the shoreline
I hang on that way

I am something of a better man
Existing under your full canopy of light
Lately love,
It's the only way I know how to survive

Don't bother with the bodies in the dark
They're only there to remind me
Of the short distance between
The old me and your heart

TO MY CHILD

You will have lonesome dreams
You will wake up sweating
Afraid of losing—
Losing yourself really
Not so much everyone else

You will develop disorders my love
We all do
Growing up is about eating
And keeping it down

I wish someone had told me that
I wish someone had said Son
You will hurt
You will be so soggy on some days
That it feels as if the world
Wants you to return to it
Through the earth
To a seed
Disappearing
Until you have disappeared completely

But it's all not so final
I promise
And to my future daughter
My little seed
When the world tells you
To be anything
When it tortures you
Remember,
That you are
Only as fragile
As you allow yourself to be

SEED

None of you
Were born anything other
Than a seed
And if you have a son
He will begin as
None other than a seed
If you have a daughter
She will begin as
None other than a seed

There is ministry
In understanding the simple things

<u>CLICHE</u>

I am sick and tired of reading it!
You are not a beautiful chaos
You are not a violent tornado
Ripping through hearts to save your own
You are not some damsel in distress
Pricking your fingers
With the thorns of unworthy lovers

You are a sanctuary
Not some young poet's hobby
Who—by the way
Would so quickly believe
That love is born
From between your legs!

You my dear are a vow
Something permanent that
Permeates the universe
Hell—
Your hands hold the shape of the earth

JUST ANOTHER BREATH
IN A HEAVING WORLD

It's quiet this time of morning
My wrists understand the language
Yet
Remain languid in their love

Nothing is staved in
As the dreams of children
Head north from the harbors
With my mind moored to some
Weathered wharf

Moss grows in the dark
Most things take shape when we ignore them

The lips of rotation
Expose the light
And the kiss of dawn
Stirs—
Orphaned stubbornness
Is breaking through falsely created truths
And feet will soon blemish this day
Bodies wake
And drag such heavy gloom
In their shadowy weight

O' what is there to teach my sorrow
When my fingertips are such cowards?

Northern expansion met with light
And my dark will damn it by closing lids
Most days I'm a deserter to my own existence
A secondary color in a rainbow
Just another breath in a heaving world

D E A D W O O D

Quick hands polishing the sky
I've been up all night
Watching concrete workers
Watching cigarette smokers
Watching drunken patrons spill into cars

It's laborious to imagine myself among them
With the calendar hanging me in so many ways

Instead I slope in defiance of that mountain
Strip naked, finally rich with freedom—
With guile
And swim
In retreat of every firecracker memory
Exhausting my muscles until I cramp
As if the body was reshaping itself
Embryonically

Lungs beg like a newborn on a Tuesday
Or a man slumped over his dying wife
I am sapped,
Enervated with giving myself away like a eulogy

The task of freeing oneself
From a free worlds mandates
Is medicinal
But more difficult
Than reigniting wet wood

But I must
For I cannot keep living out these decades
Like deadwood

ABOUT A BRUISE

These eyes have seen too many ghosts
To speak of grace
Or the value of silence

Chariot up your will
And chain it to western beliefs
The body can no longer tell
If it is a hunger or a feast

This feeble armistice is coming down
Violently—
Then all at once
A kite string laced through a Gull wing
All glances and chances
Repositioning the rust throughout the machine
Begging, literally begging
For depression to give you an identity

It's castrating, metaphorically
To be hinged to such a thing
But too often, guts hang in the belfry
While the heart aches beneath boards
And the suffering between them
Is just familiar enough to feel warm

Oh, then that fire starts in your head
Let it spread
It is pure
To feel that darkness start nesting
To cleave yourself empty

The strength of anything
Is measured by its ability to bruise

ODYSSEY

An ode to summer love
And how it marches
With two left feet

'Tis the tragedy of the
marigold
To bloom feverishly
In blessed heat
Just to perish
Under winter's snowy sheet

Yet the brain can't help but
drift aside
To thoughts of the fruit fly
And what it may think
Of such a timeline?

Often we exhaust the soul
By dooming the heart
To siphoned swings
Of happiness or melancholy
When really
One should cherish experience
Even trysts that occur
perennially
For love, like life
Is often more an odyssey

ODYSSEY (BY BEN PEDARY)

See how pastures burn
To give new grass its turn

What clears the weeds
And nurtures the earth
Doesn't diminish the prairies' worth

Drink the inferno, digest the ash
Bitter syrup to ease the backlash

Color yourself on crimson pages
Scratch at walls to find reason
Such beauty in songs we bleed
To stride this path for even a sea-
son

Stripped-down reality
Over wishes on Big Dipper
Beats the drunken walk through
Glass dreams on glass slippers

CRACKS

I believe that these
Cracks in me
Have turned into valleys

In that
I know
That loneliness
Shall
Never leave me lonely

HARD TO BE THE ONE STILL ALIVE

I'm still gestating my pain
It's been a few years
Since the daisy didn't bloom
And after a heavy rain
The soil looks like
The dog was foolishly digging

I used to believe in my submerged movements
Of helplessness blues
Pen stroked elegies to fill the hole in my luck
And my lung
Soft breaths read the list of names
As I drink nightmares through swirls of gray
Swaddled in the base of tomorrow
Still reverberating from yesterday

It's a strange thing
To belong to buried bodies
Something with invisible hands
Lately I've been feeling
Like the ashes of a better man

Bereavement resurrected
An asterisk placed against the palate
When those vowels and consonants try to flank it
I'm out of place
As clocks measure distance from,
As opposed to toward
And the drain is accosting

As I recoil and display
A lack of pride in my skinny veins

What happened to pace?
The tachypnea proxies' art
For a shipwreck of unspeakable things
And the swell had been seething inside this body

The pen wrote me into the soil
And I can see no decay
As I'm standing next to you
I'm both relieved and flattened

You are alive
Preserved in the bits that my soul refuses to digest
You are alive

MURPHY

I want to be dead weight
The tyranny to your fantasy
A gypsy memory
With a fake history
Drinking sweat through
A day old daisy stem

I cannot stand the taste of time
Or kitchen silence—
It leaks from empty Tupperware
Containers, containing
Much of who I was
And who I am to be

I hate residue
It is all sessions, scars, and seasons
The weight of which is trafficked along
Courteous smiles
Held like a pin in my palm
        In the dark relapses of my mind

There is a railroad in a tunnel
And I stand here with concrete feet
Reciting,
My name is Murphy
        Come set me free

DEFINING DEPRESSION

I tried to kill myself once
It was hard to talk about
It was the hardest thing I've ever had to write about

It wasn't about you
Or my disjointed family
It wasn't about love
Or the lack of
It was about blood loss—
Mine.
It was about me.

See--
Depression is a blank slate
And the problem is
That is all it will ever feel like
Regardless
Of the color of the paint
Used to define the mess

People mistakenly quantify sadness
As a morose sense of self indulgence
It isn't. It isn't.

LIVING AND MOLTING AND LIVING

Please keep your hands out of pools you don't
understand. Nature is a beast not meant for weak
hearted humans. The golden rule will not apply to
soft spoken souls. Love is just infliction of
circumstance and we all inhale it, To take another
shot of life.
In us—little exhibits exist in ten year increments
And then we shed our skin.
Molting under the light of hierarchy and a chance
at heaven. What a grave mistake. To live just for the
sake of it.
Life is nothing more than an excuse to die.
Slowly, but it is.
Profound or profane
Really it's the same.
Every moment is virgin and the accumulation of time
Can truly happen in an instant.
We are all combusting and erupting
That my friends is living.
Quit aching for that next day swoon.
The arc of midnight is approaching
And we all have a chance to swing from the moon.

DEFINING ART

I have a clever mouth
Trust me
I have tasted guilt and didn't spit it out

How else do you think
I learned that art is not rebellion of the mind
But rather the misfortune
Of a mischievous heart

DEPLOYMENT

She lingers in me
The way the gospel was supposed to
And I can't seem to articulate
How I grasped the concept of fate
As the sounds you made
Vibrated our weight

I wish the sun pouring in
Could have bleached this past year
Into our sheets
Because it's so hard to find you
Each morning
When I can't clutch your hand
In the interim of my waking

You are significant
Even though you aren't present
You are here
I'm just struggling to hear
The voice I've honed my ears
To listen for my whole life

And in this temporary misery
I am still happy
Knowing you will return to me
My love
I am not simply patient
I am in love

LOVE CAN BE AN F WORD

My God
How you tip my anxious heart
And tempt my fingers
To move through your creases
Until they belong to an ocean

Syllables that have never been conceived
Before this moment
Are given a birthday
And a first name

The sunlight becomes calligraphic
Inscribing the steps of our motion
Into the carpet

I used to be afraid
To write fuck in my poems
But that was before you
Before it had such a sweet connotation
And I'm not scared anymore

S H A M A N

Deft love
A sure thing
Like candy on Halloween

Before it
I dressed up my axiomatic heart
For what seemed like a hundred years
Claiming that it was some descendant
Of nocturnal intimacy
The stillness of drying wax
That blushed the maniacal hands of marooned spirits
around me

Suddenly
A manifestation of sound
Burst like acoustics
After a cochlear implant
You were my surgery,
Stitching whispers from the sun
Into my abdomen
Instead of attempting to remove
The shadows cast from decades of plump dejection

You were a shaman with sure hands
And I swear I never thought myself a patient man
But it took 29 years to find your hand

WALK AWAY

Find the will
To love
But find the strength
To walk away
If it does not
Love you back

WRITING LEFT HANDED

You paralyze me
Carelessly
Taxing my skin
To keep my doubtfully growing bones in

I needed to sink
When you needed structure
I used to spend long nights
Battling which person had it harder

Falling apart isn't as easy as it seems
Have you ever tried to let go of something?
It's like holding
A snowflake on your tongue
Without melting

But I also broke my finger once
And recall learning to write with my left hand
Teaching myself to rely on the unfamiliar
Was woefully complex
And my signature has not been the same since

But I am better for it

THE DEATH OF A GLORIOUS GESTALT

There are distant memories
Of you showing your strength
And flashing your teeth
It's so conflicting
As you measure up to bones softening
A marriage of syrup and desire

We burn like a match in winter
And I come apart
Like napkins in water
That kind of separating is more painful
Than immediate displacement
        (I can promise you that)

I studied the fray
After I witnessed the death
Of a glorious gestalt
I took a holiday from inevitability—
It concreted me to stubbornness

I used to honor my volition
And actuality

So much so that I detached
No longer throned to your side
I swear on the stars
In those coffee eyes
That I'd go blind
To be bound again

It seems I keep forcing my toes
Into the same sand we sunk in
Before we were sinking in sand
And all I have left
Are these blistered hands

TENDRILS OF OPHELIA

The tendrils of Ophelia are surrendering
To the prisms of me
I am a pillar of some decade old reflection
A vagrant in all of my vulnerability

HAPPINESS

How much
Of your own happiness
Will be determined
By the pursuit of it?

THE COLLISION OF PHYSICAL AND METAPHYSICAL

Our cells converged
And I felt the whiplash
Something about your hips
Gave me a timeline
For where my world ends

You were born with heavens
On both hemispheres

It's not your fault
That your perfection
Doesn't stutter
But rather—
Forces people to pay attention

Feathered between my two hands
I will have you unlearn the names
Of every former lover
Tonight

DEFINING FRAGILITY

Fragile things
Make up
What they lack in strength
In what they teach

THE OCEAN GREW HANDS

You're not out of the lake yet son
Stillborn thoughts are still littering
The space between your heart and tongue
Quit dragging the floor for bodies
And start digging underneath
For an ocean that will grow hands

There is this nagging miracle
From a time ago
Where I created teeth
And a goddamned heartbeat
Before I named fall the season
Of paper lanterns

It's a strange thing to gain greater sight
Through the experience of loss
It's an awful thing to move on
And feels even worse to forgive yourself for it

U N B O R N

Little Lungs
Always at rest

You are a gun
That will never know death

Damaged digits
Arching blonde curls
Simple miracle laid to rest
Among tidal pearls

O' cruel fate
The most accurate pain
Has shaky aim

THE SON THAT NEVER UNDERSTOOD

I thought I bloomed
To some staircase descending
But it really all depended
On how the lens was leaning

Scoured four years from birth
I saw the spit turn into oceans
As my shell cracked like a pistachio
On the end table
And all I'm remembering
Was how red sheets
Remind me of your walking away
30 years later—I don't own any

I hope you never have to know
How I am haunted by what I may have said
To make you lose your humanity—
I don't love you anymore
Though I swear I did then,
        At least I think I did then

Later that year
Weak eyed, I asked my preacher
Why flowers grow thorns?
I recall the recitation of some perfumed scripture
About universal love
And how we belong to welcomed gates above
Yet—
God drowned the world
Including all those flowers with thorns

Maybe I was asking the wrong questions,
Maybe I've been asking all the wrong questions all
along

GRISELDA MOODS

You held that Styrofoam between your teeth
A backwards filling scrapping
Beneath those maple trees
Constantly chopping at those heavy storms
In your nightmares
Gathering, like dirty laundry

We traveled acid drips and axe tips
Witnesses to our own shame
And slept in until June
Look what blackberry porter lips did to you
Look what they did to me!

Lemon and plaid
Waltzing that neon smoke of young love
Quietly perching
On houses we would point at
From the middle of the street
Saying things with un-pinched cheeks,
Like—

"We'll never live here, but everyone is pretending
anyways"

If corn is sugar and sugar is saccharine
Then
It's possible we're not all that different
From the artifice we've been existing in

Griselda moods, I loved us then
Even with that hollow boxing from within
You saw coal, while I was staring at diamonds

WHY I DON'T DONATE BLOOD

These days
I feel numb to it all
There's not a song
That can levy the tide against the storm

This swell of bad behavior
Is bone deep and broken
Sharing coding from baby birds
That found their beaks against a window
Far too young

We have the same blood
I don't donate
For that reason
There's trouble in explaining
The harvest to the hostage—

Every dark shift in this room
Is a person that I once knew

I can't swallow
What can't swallow me
Repeat; Repeat
Ruin myself repeating
Ruin myself believing

Castles fall when the basket is emptied of all its
arrows
And my edges have been dull for years
Love is merely a weight
Holding me in place
And as I've gladly surrendered to the scent of it
When it washes off
I shall disappear

MOVE FORWARD

At days wink
We are all well-known strangers
The pupils of good pain
The hands of challengers
Fighting for the morning
After a strong rain

LIFE CYCLES OF LOVE

Your body will take the blame
For the confessions from fake lighting
Pouring
Over late night lovers
That leave your sheets feeling
Like a hotel shared with a stranger

You heart will play Mozart
A thousand times louder
Than it should
When you see the lashes
Of someone real
Rise from hibernation
> *And you will rise with them*

You will run away with your youth
To the mouths that taste like fruit

It's only normal
To break some bones while you grow
It's only normal
To find your way home through
The thick wickets of better bruises
Before you finally reach
Deep pools of love

DROWNING OR WORSE

The problem
With appreciating the rain
Or anything
Visually stunning
Is the potential
Of drowning
Or worse
        Falling in love

FLESH

The fault in our flesh
Rests in our desire for it

WHO TO BELIEVE

I was told to believe in my parents
When I was young
But old crock pot meals
And weak fisted apologies
Changed me

I was told to believe in God
So I gave my time
And bent knees
To stained glass pictures
Of a long haired man
Who eventually damned me
To just another vacancy

I was told to believe in teachers
And they taught me a lot about planning
Though it was more about the rejection
That I retained

I was told to believe in love
And I gave
      And gave
            And gave
Until love couldn't

Then I was told to believe in myself
And I wanted to
But as I dug my hands into the soil of my soul
No seeds were there

I had already given so much away
To everyone that was supposed to nourish me
That nothing was left to nurture
Or grow

Empty and wiser
This is the only message I have left to offer
Grow from within
Before you extend
To satisfy the opinions of others

SUICIDE STIGMA

I'm not supposed to talk about it
I'm supposed to stand here
And explain how I've moved mountains
How I've built fucking spaceships and trains
Out of shattered tectonic plates

How I've conjured loss
And the sexual burglary
Witnessed by a six year old's brain
And dug down to a more fertile place
To grow something beautiful from that pain

The thing is I didn't!
I've been a liar for far too long

I tried to join that chain gang in the sky
I tried to shake hands with angels
So I could see my brother smile
One more time

I tried to kill myself

I say it out loud
And I think of my wife
How she loves every piece
To include that one

      That brings me peace

I think of all the things
I would have missed
Had I gone through with it
Yet—I'm not supposed to talk about it?

GONE WITH THE OCEAN

There is a calendar eye shuttering
At the snarling gargoyle print
Stretching across the carpet
Pregnant with air pockets—it groans
As Transatlanticism plays on the radio

The footprints of the eldest child
Shadow the corner where he used to sit
What once was punishment,
Parents now kneel around it

It's sad how we become the tide
Especially, and typically when
We don't talk about the ocean

We hold things just close enough
To let them go
And be okay with it.

Until they are gone that is

EAGER LOVE

The problem
With
Eager love
Is
It will
Empty you
To fill
The other up

HUNGER PAINS

Sometimes
Love is just a gutter dog
Looking for its last meal

Don't confuse
Happiness with forever

Life is anything but linear!

THIS IS IT

This is it
Happiness
Or the end

Eukaryotic and I accept it
My descent was not propaganda
I was born with a trigger finger
And a gun at my head

Embryonic
Something in the blood I suppose
A violator that climbed in
During the plagues
When Christ was a fleshy being
That others were hooked and hammered for
following

Not much has changed
Except for the miracles we beg to emerge
From the hearts we have banished into tombs
Except for the beliefs we subscribe to
That end up hanging our octaves and lungs
Across plunging rooms

I inhale the repose of it all
Death
Soil
Bad poets

My overworked shoulder blades are soaking in the
ocean
And it has been eternities sine I met a wave
That could simultaneously
Paralyze and offer suspension
I was committed to depression
That was, until love gave me a chance
And I'm enamored with my backwards walk
A handsome way of comprehending
The sovereignties in surrendering

Yet, still
Even in rewind the truth is the same
And the wasp may not love honey
Though it can grasp the drive of bees
It is in these essential intricacies
That make us much more than biology

I am dampening this self-apology
Today is more than my history
It's reaching out with the hand not holding the gun
It's faith, admission and glorifying hope
I can cope. I can cope. I can cope.

I am as much my own captor
As I am my own savior

Hang on
Or hang on just long enough.

M A D   O N E

I'm exhausted
From throwing stones at reflections
Pretending the ripples
Are distorted images
Of decomposing and composing again

Like a morning without stars
The forgotten hours
       I know these roads
Like the leaves on the side of them

We should shed our teeth
And smoke out our heads
There are months to come
Where we won't need them

I'll spend desperate days in bed
Feeding off of our sex
Leaving marks on your excitement
Until the fabric of my pull
Becomes a boring shove away

Mad one, she'll say
You've got no understanding
Of love
You haven't made me breakfast
Or coffee in weeks
You do nothing
But fuck your sadness into me

And I used to be able to hold it
Now I'm losing my sanity
I thought there'd be a vacancy
That my spirit could inhabit eventually
But now I think it's crippling

We've become nothing
But smoke caught in a cloche
Held together by suction
And
Mad one,
I'm leaving

MADNESS

I used
To take my madness
For granted

That was
Until I
Took the time
To understand it

PASSION

Find a passion
That exhausts your pain

I promise you then
Everything will be okay

FATE

An illusionist's trick
The greatest ever pulled
Was re-gifting grief
To the person who sullied me

Distant father
Where are your tinsel hands now?

As the lamb was birthed beneath a steeple
To live within a cloche
You were nowhere to be found

The bliss of music was coated in pollen
And contained no sound

With a stunted spine
I hoarded oxygen
Inside of frail lungs
And never grew into a cardinal direction
Somehow that was my fault?

Foul
    Trident tipped tongue
I drip
    And drip
         And
Condensate like rain
On plagues of the young
Outcasts with the volume up (For decades now)
And the hoards will rise
To burn the lianas covering the clock

Our time begins again
Again, our time begins

So Father,
I'd presume you dead
Before I tell you about
The Holy Mountain I have climbed
But what if this triumph
Was fated the whole time?

THE MAN WHO DROWNED
HIMSELF ON STAGE

Soft moon riding shotgun to the quotient of a
daydream. A mangled ocean painted in patient
strokes above me, reflecting a patriarchal line of Irish
iris.
The sins of my father sit pleated above my big toe,
But he wouldn't be able to remember them.
Not anymore.

I am barely a synonym for heir these days. Anyways.
The sun permeates and walks my skin like tiny ants

I think to myself,
"This must be how people heal. Normal people"
The calm is a slow motion dance of a bride in a loch.
Some smooth address to fragile eyes.
The attention of furloughed ambition.
I would clamor at the chance to feel this again.
Though this body has accepted that relief comes in
chances and moments
Reverence is married to a different suitor
Whereas to my misfortune, I am a monogamist.

Geese pull their gander to the far side of the hill,
And I am alone again
In both stupor and grandeur.

I sip my coffee.
Today my poetry will undress me,
On this stage
Soaking in the majesty of a soft room
It will end.

ACKNOWLEDGEMENTS

Thank you to my wife for not letting my light burn out. Without your nudging I wouldn't have published a damn thing.

Thank you to Ben Pedary for providing your piece (Odyssey) on Pg. 109. It's a true pleasure to create art with genuine people who recognize the power in its purpose.

Thank you to my friends and family who may not always understand my writing, but still support it.

Thank you to my history, and to my future.

ABOUT THE AUTHOR

Patrick David Hart is an American writer that finds therapeutic value in acknowledging truths that most hide from. The majority of his work is steeped in personal experience, which is where he pulls his inspiration from. You can find more of his work in his other book, WAR PAINT, or on Instagram @workinprogressl3.